BRIDAL BOUQUET

PENHALIGON'S
SCENTED TREASURY OF
VERSE AND PROSE

BRIDAL
BOUQUET

EDITED BY SHEILA PICKLES

HARMONY BOOKS

To my bridesmaids
Alice, Grace and Claire

CONTENTS

INTRODUCTION

Dear Reader,

A wedding is many things, foremost a declaration of love and dedication, a union celebrated by every culture since time immemorial. The many elements of the modern wedding ceremony are rooted in magic and paganism: the veil, an image of chastity; the flowers, emblems of fertility; and the ring, a symbol of love and dedication based on the ancient idea that a vein runs from the fourth finger to the heart.

Marriage has been celebrated in many novels and poems. Throughout literature, relationships between humble cottagers, lords and ladies, princes and princesses have progressed through the crescendo of courtship and engagement towards the final happy ending of an announcement of marriage, and the wedding. In this anthology I have selected some passages from my favourite poetry and prose on the theme of betrothal.

Becoming engaged is a moment when dreams become reality. This is something which literally happens to Keats' heroine Madeline who wakes from a reverie on the magical St Agnes' Eve to find her lover Porphyro in her moonlit chamber. Some of you will feel, like Elizabeth von Arnim's heroine, Catherine, that your inner happiness shines through to make you feel like a new person. You may have a ring slipped onto your finger, or perhaps be bound by some other token like a bracelet, which Herrick describes so eloquently in his verse to Julia. Some of you may opt for a quiet village wedding, others may choose a much grander venue – but whichever it is, may your day be an occasion of great joy and unforgettable memories.

Scented with the fragrance of Orange Blossom and illustrated with beautiful period paintings, *Bridal Bouquet* is for all brides, and an evocative celebration of the traditions and romance of marriage.

Sheila Pickles
London 1991

PROPOSALS

A SINGLE MAN

*I*T IS a truth universally acknowledged, that a single man in possession of a good fortune must be in want of a wife.

However little known the feelings or views of such a man may be on his first entering a neighbourhood, this truth is so well fixed in the minds of the surrounding families, that he is considered as the rightful property of someone or other of their daughters.

"My dear Mr. Bennet," said his lady to him one day, "have you heard that Netherfield Park is let at last?"

Mr. Bennet replied that he had not.

"But it is," returned she, "for Mrs. Long has just been here, and she told me all about it."

"Do not you want to know who has taken it?" cried his wife impatiently.

"*You* want to tell me, and I have no objection to hearing it."

"Why, my dear, you must know. Mrs. Long says that Netherfield is taken by a young man of large fortune from the north of England; that he came down on Monday in a chaise and four to see the place, and was so much delighted with it, that he agreed with Mr. Morris immediately; that he is to take possession before Michaelmas, and some of his servants are to be in the house by the end of next week."

"What is his name?"

"Bingley."

"Is he married or single?"

"Oh! single, my dear, to be sure! A single man of large fortune; four or five thousand a year. What a fine thing for our girls!"

"How so? How can it affect them?"

"My dear Mr. Bennet," replied his wife, "how can you be so tiresome! You must know that I am thinking of his marrying one of them."

FROM *PRIDE AND PREJUDICE* BY JANE AUSTEN, 1775-1817

THE PROPOSAL

"COME," said Gabriel, freshening again: "think a minute or two. I'll wait a while, Miss Everdene. Will you marry me? Do, Bathsheba. I love you far more than common!"

"I'll try to think," she observed rather more timorously; "if I can think out of doors; my mind spreads away so."

"But you can give a guess."

"Then give me time." Bathsheba looked thoughtfully into the distance, away from the direction in which Gabriel stood.

"I can make you happy," said he to the back of her head, across the bush. "You shall have a piano in a year or two – farmers' wives are getting to have pianos now – and I'll practise up the flute right well to play with you in the evenings."

"Yes, I should like that."

"And have one of those little ten-pound gigs for market – and nice flowers, and birds – cocks and hens I mean, because they be useful," continued Gabriel, feeling balanced between poetry and practicality.

"I should like it very much."

"And a frame for cucumbers – like a gentleman and lady."

"Yes."

"And when the wedding was over, we'd have it put in the newspaper list of marriages."

"Dearly I should like that!"

"And the babies in the births – every man jack of 'em! And at home by the fire, whenever you look up, there I shall be – and whenever I look up, there will be you."

"Wait, wait, and don't be improper!"

Her countenance fell, and she was silent awhile. He regarded the red berries between them over and over again, to such an extent that holly seemed in his after life to be a cypher signifying a proposal of marriage. Bathsheba decisively turned to him.

"No; 'tis no use," she said. "I don't want to marry you."

FROM *FAR FROM THE MADDING CROWD* BY THOMAS HARDY, 1840-1928

INNOCENCE

OROTHEA, with all her eagerness to know the truths of life, retained very childlike ideas about marriage. She felt sure that she would have accepted the judicious Hooker, if she had been born in time to save him from that wretched mistake he made in matrimony; or John Milton when his blindness had come on; or any of the other great men whose odd habits it would have been glorious piety to endure; but an amiable handsome baronet, who said "Exactly" to her remarks even when she expressed uncertainty, – how could he affect her as a lover? The really delightful marriage must be that where your husband was a sort of father, and could teach you even Hebrew, if you wished it. . . .

And how should Dorothea not marry? – a girl so handsome and with such prospects? Nothing could hinder it but her love of extremes, and her insistence on regulating life according to notions which might cause a wary man to hesitate before he made her an offer, or even might lead her at last to refuse all offers. A young lady of some birth and fortune, who knelt suddenly down on a brick floor by the side of a sick labourer and prayed fervidly as if she thought herself living in the time of the Apostles – who had strange whims of fasting like a Papist, and of sitting up at night to read old theological books! Such a wife might awaken you some fine morning with a new scheme for the application of her income which would interfere with political economy and the keeping of saddle-horses: a man would naturally think twice before he risked himself in such fellowship. Women were expected to have weak opinions; but the great safeguard of society and of domestic life was, that opinions were not acted on. Sane people did what their neighbours did, so that if any lunatics were at large, one might know and avoid them.

FROM *MIDDLEMARCH* BY GEORGE ELIOT, 1819-1880

THE CONFESSION

"WELL?" Darius growled impatiently, even savagely. They saw each other, not once a week, but at nearly every hour of every day, and they were surfeited of the companionship.

"Supposing I wanted to get married?" This sentence shot out of Edwin's mouth like a bolt. And as it flew, he blushed very red. In the privacy of his mind he was horribly swearing.

"So that's it, is it?" Darius growled again. And he leaned forward and picked up the poker, not as a menace, but because he too was nervous. As an opposer of his son he had never had quite the same confidence in himself since Edwin's historic fury at being suspected of theft, though apparently their relations had resumed the old basis of bullying and submission.

"Well –" Edwin hesitated. He thought, "after all, people do get married. It won't be a crime."

"Who'st been running after?" Darius demanded inimically. Instead of being softened by this rumour of love, by this hint that his son had been passing through wondrous secret hours, he instinctively and without any reason hardened himself and transformed the news into an offence. He felt no sympathy and it did not occur to him to recall that he too had once thought of marrying. He was a man whom life had brutalized about half a century earlier.

"I was only thinking," said Edwin clumsily – the fool had not sense enough even to sit down – "I was only thinking, suppose I *did* want to get married."

"Who'st been running after?"

"Well, I can't rightly say there's anything – what you may call settled. In fact, nothing was to be said about it all at present. But it's Miss Lessways, father – Hilda Lessways, you know."

"Her as came in the shop the other day?"

"Yes."

"How long's this been going on?"

Edwin thought of what Hilda had said, "Oh! Over a year." He could not possibly have said "four days". "Mind you this is strictly q.t.! Nobody knows a word about it, nobody! But of course I thought I'd better tell you. You'll say nothing." He tried wistfully to appeal as one loyal man to another. But he failed. There was no ray of response on his father's gloomy features, and he slipped back insensibly into the boy whose right to an individual existence had never been formally admitted.

Something base in him – something of that baseness which occasionally actuates the oppressed – made him add: "She's got an income of her own. Her father left money." He conceived that this would placate Darius.

"I know all about her father," Darius sneered, with a short laugh. "And her father's father! ... Well, lad, ye'll go your own road." He appeared to have no further interest in the affair.

FROM *CLAYHANGER* BY ARNOLD BENNETT, 1867-1931

THE BRACELET TO JULIA

WHY I tye about thy wrist,
    Julia, this my silken twist ;
    For what other reason is 't,
But to shew thee how in part
Thou my pretty captive art ?
But thy bond-slave is my heart ;
'Tis but silke that bindeth thee.

Knap the thread and thou art free ;
But 'tis otherwise with me ;
I am bound, and fast bound so,
That from thee I cannot go ;
If I co'd, I wo'd not so.

ROBERT HERRICK, 1591-1674

A Direct Question

"I HAVE one question to put to you," said Mademoiselle de Fontaine, trembling, and with a voice full of emotion, after a long silence, and after they had taken a few slow steps forward; but I beg you to consider, that it is in some sort forced upon me, by the very strange position in which I am placed with regard to my family."

A pause that was terrible to Emilie succeeded these words, which she had uttered with something approaching a stammer. During the time occupied by this pause, this proud young woman did not dare to encounter the ardent gaze of the man she loved, for she had a secret consciousness of the baseness of the ensuing words, as she added, "Are you of noble birth?" . . .

"I have no titles to offer to my wife," he replied, with an air half gay, half serious. "But if I take her from a high position, and from among those whose father's wealth has made luxury and the pleasures of opulence habitual to them, I know the duty which my choice imposes on me. Love gives all," he added gaily, "but only to lovers, – as to married folks, they need something more than the dome of heaven and the carpets of the meadows."

FROM *LE BAL DE SCEAUX* BY HONORÉ DE BALZAC, 1799-1850

On a Splendud Match

*H*E WAS warned against the *womern* –
    She was warned aginst the *man*. –
    And ef *that* won't make a weddin',
W'y, they's nothin' else that can !

JAMES WHITCOMB RILEY

TO SILVIA TO WED

*L*ET US, though late, at last, my Silvia, wed;
   And loving lie in one devoted bed.
   Thy watch may stand, my minutes fly post haste;
No sound calls back the yeere that once is past.
Then sweetest Silvia, let's no longer stay;
True love, we know, precipitates delay.
Away with doubts, all scruples hence remove;
No man, at one time, can be wise, and love.

ROBERT HERRICK, 1591-1674

Words of Wisdom

"WHAT ideas have they been filling your head with, you young girls of to-day?"

Berthe replied:

"But marriage is sacred, grandmamma."

The grandmother's heart, which had its birth in the great age of gallantry, gave a sudden leap.

"It is love that is sacred," she said. "Listen child, to an old woman who has seen three generations, and who has had a long, long experience of men and women. Marriage and love have nothing in common. We marry to found a family, and we form families in order to constitute society. Society cannot dispense with marriage. If society is a chain, each family is a link in that chain. In order to weld those links, we always seek for metals of the same kind. When we marry, we must bring the same conventions together; we must combine fortunes, unite similar races, and aim at the common interest, which is riches and children. We marry only once, my child, because the world requires us to do so, but we may love twenty times in one lifetime because nature has so made us. Marriage, you see, is law, and love is an instinct, which impels us sometimes along a straight and sometimes along a crooked path. The world has made laws to combat our instincts – it was necessary to make them; but our instincts are always stronger, and we ought not to resist them too much, because they come from God, while the laws only come from men. If we did not perfume life with love, as much love as possible, darling, as we put sugar into medicines for children, nobody would care to take it just as it is."

Berthe opened her eyes widely in astonishment. She murmured:

"Oh! grandmamma, we can only love once."

FROM *A GRANDMOTHER'S ADVICE* BY GUY DE MAUPASSANT, 1850-1893

THE BRIDE OF ABYDOS

"   *Z*ULEIKA! child of gentleness!
How dear this very day must tell,
When I forget my own distress,
In losing what I love so well,
To bid thee with another dwell:
Another! and a braver man
Was never seen in battle's van.
We Moslem reck not much of blood;
But yet the line of Carasman
Unchanged, unchangeable hath stood
First of the bold Timariot bands
That won and well can keep their lands.
Enough that he who comes to woo
Is kinsman of the Bey Oglou:
His years need scarce a thought employ;
I would not have thee wed a boy.
And thou shalt have a noble dower:
And his and my united power
Will laugh to scorn the death firman,
Which others tremble but to scan,
And teach the messenger what fate
The bearer of such boon may wait,
And now thou know'st thy father's will:
All that thy sex hath need to know;
'Twas mine to teach obedience still –
The way to love, thy lord may show."

LORD BYRON, 1788-1824

IN LOVE WITH UNDINE SPRAGG

*H*is mother and sister of course wanted him to marry. They had the usual theory that he was "made" for conjugal bliss: women always thought that of a fellow who didn't get drunk and have low tastes. Ralph smiled at the idea as he sat crouched among his secret treasures. Marry – but whom, in the name of light and freedom? The daughters of his own race sold themselves to the Invaders; the daughters of the Invaders bought their husbands as they bought an opera-box. It ought all to have been transacted on the Stock Exchange. His mother, he knew, had no such ambitions for him: she would have liked him to fancy a "nice girl" like Harriet Ray. Harriet Ray was neither vulgar nor ambitious. She regarded Washington Square as the birth-place of Society, knew by heart all the cousinships of early New York, hated motor-cars, could not make herself under-stood on the telephone, and was determined, if she married, never to receive a divorced woman. As Mrs. Marvell often said, such girls as Harriet were growing rare. Ralph was not sure about this. He was inclined to think that, certain modifications allowed for, there would always be plenty of Harriet Rays for unworldly mothers to commend to their sons; and he had no desire to diminish their number by removing one from the ranks of the marriageable. He had no desire to marry at all – that had been the whole truth of it till he met Undine Spragg. And now –? He lit a cigar, and began to recall his hour's conversation with Mrs Spragg.

FROM *THE CUSTOM OF THE COUNTRY* BY EDITH WHARTON, 1862-1937

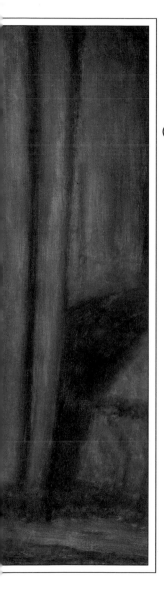

THE EVE OF ST. AGNES

*F*ULL on this casement shone the wintry moon,
　And threw warm gules on Madeline's fair breast,
　　As down she knelt for heaven's grace and boon;
Rose-bloom fell on her hands, together prest,
And on her silver cross soft amethyst,
And on her hair a glory, like a saint:
She seem'd a splendid angel, newly drest,
Save wings, for heaven: – Porphyro grew faint:
She knelt, so pure a thing, so free from mortal taint.

Anon his heart revives: her vespers done,
Of all its wreathed pearls her hair she frees;
Unclasps her warmed jewels one by one;
Loosens her fragrant bodice; by degrees
Her rich attire creeps rustling to her knees:
Half-hidden, like a mermaid in sea-weed,
Pensive awhile she dreams awake, and sees,
In fancy, fair St. Agnes in her bed,
But dares not look behind, or all the charm is fled.

"My Madeline! sweet dreamer! lovely bride!
Say, may I be for aye thy vassal blest?
Thy beauty's shield, heart-shaped and vermeil dyed?
Ah, silver shrine, here will I take my rest
After so many hours of toil and quest,
A famish'd pilgrim, – saved by miracle.
Though I have found, I will not rob thy nest
Saving of thy sweet self; if thou think'st well
To trust, fair Madeline, to no rude infidel.

JOHN KEATS, 1795-1821

31

ENGAGEMENT

CATHERINE IN LOVE

ETWEEN the end of March, when these things happened, and the end of April, when Catherine married Christopher, all taxi-drivers, bus-conductors and railway-porters called her Miss.

Such was the effect Christopher had on her. Except for him, she reflected, they probably would have addressed her as Mother, for except for him she would have been profoundly miserable at this time, in the deep disgrace and pain of being cut off from Virginia, from whom her letters came back unopened, re-addressed by Stephen; and there was nothing like inward misery, she knew, for turning women into apparent mothers, old mothers, just as there was nothing like inward happiness for turning them into apparent misses, young misses. She had this inward happiness, for she had Christopher to love her, to comfort her, to feed her with sweet names; and she flowered in his warmth into a beauty she had never possessed in the tepid days of George. Obviously what the world needed was love. She couldn't help thinking this when she caught sight of her own changed face in the glass.

FROM *LOVE* BY ELIZABETH VON ARNIM, 1866-1941

LUCY AS A WORK OF ART

A FEW days after the engagement was announced Mrs. Honeychurch made Lucy and her Fiasco come to a little garden party in the neighbourhood, for naturally she wanted to show people that her daughter was marrying a presentable man.

Cecil was more than presentable; he looked distinguished, and it was very pleasant to see his slim figure keeping step with Lucy, and his long, fair face responding when Lucy spoke to him. People congratulated Mrs. Honeychurch, which is, I believe, a social blunder, but it pleased her, and she introduced Cecil rather indiscriminately to some stuffy dowagers.

At tea a misfortune took place: a cup of coffee was upset over Lucy's figured silk, and though Lucy feigned indifference her mother feigned nothing of the sort, but dragged her indoors to have the frock treated by a sympathetic maid. They were gone some time, and Cecil was left with the dowagers. When they returned he was not as pleasant as he had been.

"Do you go to much of this sort of thing?" he asked when they were driving home.

"Oh, now and then," said Lucy, who had rather enjoyed herself.

"Is it typical of county society?"

"I suppose so. Mother, would it be?"

"Plenty of society," said Mrs. Honeychurch, who was trying to remember the hang of one of the dresses.

Seeing that her thoughts were elsewhere, Cecil bent towards Lucy and said:

"To me it seemed perfectly appalling, disastrous, portentous."

"I am so sorry that you were stranded."

"Not that, but the congratulations. It is so disgusting, the way an engagement is regarded as public property – a kind of waste place where every outsider may shoot his vulgar sentiment. All those old women smirking!"

"One has to go through it, I suppose. They won't notice us so much next time."

"But my point is that their whole attitude is wrong. An engagement – horrid word in the first place – is a private matter, and should be treated as such."

Yet the smirking old women, however wrong individually, were racially correct. The spirit of the generations had smiled through them, rejoicing in the engagement of Cecil and Lucy because it promised the continuance of life on earth. To Cecil and Lucy it promised something quite different – personal love. Hence Cecil's irritation and Lucy's belief that his irritation was just.

"How tiresome!" she said. "Couldn't you have escaped to tennis?"

FROM *A ROOM WITH A VIEW* BY E.M. FORSTER. 1879-1970

ISABEL'S CHOICE

"WHY shouldn't I like Mr. Osmond, since others have done so?"

"Others, at their wildest moments, never wanted to marry him. There's nothing *of* him," Mrs. Touchett explained.

"Then he can't hurt me," said Isabel.

"Do you think you're going to be happy? No one's happy, in such doings, you should know."

"I shall set the fashion then. What does one marry for?"

"What *you* will marry for, heaven only knows. People usually marry as they go into partnership – to set up a house. But in your partnership you'll bring everything."

"Is it that Mr. Osmond isn't rich? Is that what you're talking about?" Isabel asked.

"He has no money; he has no name; he has no importance. I value such things and I have the courage to say it; I think they're very precious. Many other people think the same, and they show it. But they give some other reason."

Isabel hesitated a little. "I think I value everything that's valuable. I care very much for money, and that's why I wish Mr. Osmond to have a little."

"Give it to him then; but marry someone else."

FROM *THE PORTRAIT OF A LADY* BY HENRY JAMES, 1843-1916

THE TROUSSEAU

*S*OON afterwards the door opened and I saw a tall, thin girl of nineteen, in a long muslin dress with a gilt belt from which, I remember, hung a mother-of-pearl fan. She came in, dropped a curtsy, and flushed crimson. Her long nose, which was slightly pitted with smallpox, turned red first, and then the flush passed up to her eyes and her forehead.

"My daughter," chanted the little lady, "and, Manetchka, this is a young gentleman who has come," etc.

I was introduced, and expressed my surprise at the number of paper patterns. Mother and daughter dropped their eyes.

"We had a fair here at Ascension," said the mother; "we always buy materials at the fair, and then it keeps us busy with sewing till the next year's fair comes round again. We never put things out to be made. My husband's pay is not very ample, and we are not able to permit ourselves luxuries. So we have to make up everything ourselves."

"But who will ever wear such a number of things? There are only two of you?"

"Oh ... as though we were thinking of wearing them! They are not to be worn; they are for the trousseau!"

"Ah, *maman*, what are you saying?" said the daughter, and she crimsoned again. "Our visitor might suppose it was true. I don't intend to be married. Never!"

She said this, but at the very word "married" her eyes glowed .... Manetchka threw off her shyness for a moment and showed me the tobacco-pouch she was embroidering for her father. When I pretended to be greatly struck by her work, she flushed crimson and whispered something in her mother's ear. The latter beamed all over, and invited me to go with her to the storeroom. There I was shown five large trunks, and a number of smaller trunks and boxes.

"This is her trousseau," her mother whispered; "we made it all ourselves."

FROM *THE TALES OF CHEKHOV*, 1860-1904

THE BRIDESMAID

"I DON'T know," said Molly; "I suppose I am to be a bridesmaid; but no one has spoken to me about my dress."

"Then I shall ask your papa."

"Please, don't. He must have to spend a great deal of money just now. Besides, I would rather not be at the wedding, if they'll let me stay away."

"Nonsense child. Why, all the town would be talking of it. You must go, and you must be well dressed, for your father's sake."

But Mr. Gibson had thought of Molly's dress, although he
had said nothing about it to her. He had commissioned his
future wife to get her what was requisite: and presently a
very smart dressmaker came over from the county-town to
try on a dress, which was both so simple and so elegant as at
once to charm Molly. When it came home all ready to put on,
Molly had a private dressing-up for Miss Brownings'
benefit; and she was almost startled when she looked into the
glass, and saw the improvement in her appearance. "I
wonder if I'm pretty," thought she, "I almost think I am – in
this kind of dress I mean, of course. Betty would say, 'Fine
feathers make fine birds.'"

When she went downstairs in her bridal attire, and with
shy blushes presented herself for inspection, she was greeted
with a burst of admiration.

"Well, upon my word! I shouldn't have known you."

"You are really beautiful – isn't she, sister?" said Miss
Phoebe. "Why, my dear, if you were always dressed, you
would be prettier than your dear mamma, whom we always
reckoned so very personable."

FROM *WIVES AND DAUGHTERS* BY ELIZABETH GASKELL, 1810-1865

THE DAY

EPITHALAMION MADE AT LINCOLN'S INN

THE sun-beams in the east are spread,
   Leave, leave, fair Bride, your solitary bed,
   No more shall you return to it alone,
It nurseth sadness, and your body's print,
Like to a grave, the yielding down doth dint;
   You and your other you meet there anon;
   Put forth, put forth that warm balm-breathing thigh,
Which when next time you in these sheets will smother
There it must meet another,
   Which never was, but must be, oft, more nigh;
Come glad from thence, go gladder than you came,
Today put on perfection, and a woman's name.

JOHN DONNE, 1572-1631

MARRIAGE MORNING

*L*IGHT, so low upon earth,
 You send a flash to the sun.
 Here is the golden close of love,
 All my wooing is done.
Oh, the woods and the meadows,
 Woods where we hid from the wet,
Stiles where we stay'd to be kind,
 Meadows in which we met!
Light, so low in the vale
 You flash and lighten afar,
For this is the golden morning of love,
 And you are his morning star.
Flash, I am coming, I come,
 By meadow and stile and wood,
Oh, lighten into my eyes and my heart,
 Into my heart and my blood!
Heart, are you great enough
 For a love that never tires?
O heart, are you great enough for love?
 I have heard of thorns and briers.
Over the thorns and briers,
 Over the meadows and stiles,
Over the world to the end of it
 Flash for a million miles.

ALFRED LORD TENNYSON, 1809-1892

THE PRIMROSE-COLOURED WAISTCOAT

"HARK! Who's that?" exclaimed a small pupil-teacher, who also assisted this morning, to her great delight. She ran half-way down the stairs, and peeped round the bannister. "O, you should, you should, you should!" she exclaimed, scrambling up to the room again.

"What?" said Fancy.

"See the bridesmaids! They've just come! 'Tis wonderful, really! 'tis wonderful how muslin can be brought to it. There, they don't look a bit like themselves, but like some very rich sisters o' theirs that nobody knew they had!"

"Make 'em come up to me, make 'em come up!" cried Fancy ecstatically; and the four damsels appointed, namely, Miss Susan Dewy, Miss Bessie Dewy, Miss Vashti Sniff, and Miss Mercy Onmey, surged upstairs, and floated along the passage.

"I wish Dick would come!" was again the burden of Fancy.

The same instant a small twig and flower from the creeper outside the door flew in at the open window, and a masculine voice said, "Ready, Fancy dearest?"

"There he is, he is!" cried Fancy, tittering spasmodically, and breathing as it were for the first time that morning.

The bridesmaids crowded to the window and turned their heads in the direction pointed out, at which motion eight ear-rings all swung as one : – not looking at Dick because they particularly wanted to see him, but with an important sense of their duty as obedient ministers of the will of that apotheosised being – the Bride.

"He looks very taking!" said Miss Vashti Sniff, a young lady who blushed cream-colour and wore yellow bonnet-ribbons.

Dick was advancing to the door in a painfully new coat of shining cloth, primrose-coloured waistcoat, hat of the same painful style of newness, and with an extra quantity of whiskers shaved off his face, and his hair cut to an unwonted shortness in honour of the occasion.

FROM *UNDER THE GREENWOOD TREE* BY THOMAS HARDY, 1840-1928

— 51 —

PAMELA

*M*Y DEAR Master came to me, at entering the Chapel, and took my Hand, and led me up to the Altar. Remember, my dear Girl, whisper'd he, and be chearful. I am, I will, Sir, said I; but I hardly knew what I said; and so you may believe, when I said to Mrs. *Jewkes*, Don't leave me; pray, Mrs. *Jewkes*, don't leave me; as if I had all Confidence in her, and none where it was most due. So she kept close to me. God forgive me! but I never was so absent in my Life, as at first: Even till Mr. *Williams* had gone on in the Service, so far as to the awful Words about *requiring us, as we should answer at the dreadful Day of Judgment*; and then the solemn Words, and my Master's whispering, Mind this, my Dear, made me start. Said he, still whispering, Know *you* any Impediment? I blush'd, and said, softly, None, Sir, but my great Unworthiness.

Then follow'd the sweet Words, *Wilt thou have this Woman to thy wedded Wife*, &c. and I began to take Heart a little, when my dearest Master answer'd, audibly, to this Question, *I will*. But I could only make a Curchee, when they asked me; tho', I am sure, my Heart was readier than my Speech, and answer'd to every Article of *obey, serve, love* and *honour*.

Mr. *Peters* gave me away, and I said after Mr. *Williams*, as well as I could, as my dear Master did, with a much better Grace, the Words of Betrothment; and the Ceremony of the Ring passing next, I received the dear Favour at his worthy Hands, with a most grateful Heart; and he was pleased to say afterwards in the Chariot, that when he had done saying, *With this Ring, I thee wed*, &c. I made a Curchee, and said, Thank you, Sir. May-be, I did; for, I am sure, it was a most grateful Part of the Service; and my Heart was overwhelm'd with his Goodness, and the tender Grace wherewith he perform'd it. I was very glad, that the next Part was the Prayer, and Kneeling; for I trembled so, I could hardly stand, betwixt Fear and Delight.

The joining of our Hands afterwards, the Declaration of
our being marry'd to the few Witnesses present; for,
reckoning *Nan*, whose Curiosity would not let her stay at the
Door, they were but Mr. *Peters*, Mrs. *Jewkes*, and she; the
Blessing, the Psalm, and the subsequent Prayers, and the
concluding Exhortation, were so many beautiful, welcome
and lovely Parts of this divine Office, that my Heart began
to be delighted with them, and my Spirits to be a little freer.

SAMUEL RICHARDSON, 1689-1761

THE MARRIAGE CEREMONY

*T*HE Vested Priest before the Altar stands:
Approach, come gladly, ye prepared, in sight
Of God and chosen friends, your troth to plight
With the symbolic ring, and willing hands
Solemnly joined. Now sanctify the bands
O Father! – to the Espoused thy blessing give,
That mutually assisted they may live
Obedient, as here taught, to thy commands.
So prays the Church, to consecrate a Vow
"The which would endless matrimony make;"
Union that shadows forth and doth partake
A mystery potent human love to endow
With heavenly, each more prized for the other's sake;
Weep not, meek Bride! uplift thy timid brow.

WILLIAM WORDSWORTH, 1770-1850

THE CELEBRATION AND BLESSING
OF A MARRIAGE

EARLY beloved: We have come together in the presence of God to witness and bless the joining together of this man and this woman in Holy Matrimony. The bond and covenant of marriage was established by God in creation, and our Lord Jesus Christ adorned this manner of life by his presence and first miracle at a wedding in Cana of Galilee. It signifies to us the mystery of the union between Christ and his Church, and Holy Scripture commends it to be honored among all people.

The union of husband and wife in heart, body, and mind is intended by God for their mutual joy; for the help and comfort given one another in prosperity and adversity; and, when it is God's will, for the procreation of children and their nurture in the knowledge and love of the Lord. Therefore marriage is not to be entered into unadvisedly or lightly, but reverently, deliberately, and in accordance with the purposes for which it was instituted by God.

FROM *THE BOOK OF COMMON PRAYER* (EPISCOPAL)

A QUIET WEDDING

A VERY quiet wedding may be just as happy an omen
as one where there is more bustle and excitement,
when a solemn service seems mingled with champagne
and laughter, orange-blossoms, tears, and smiles. At least, so
Jack Ramsay and Violet thought, when in the early spring-
time they were married; and few, very few were present to

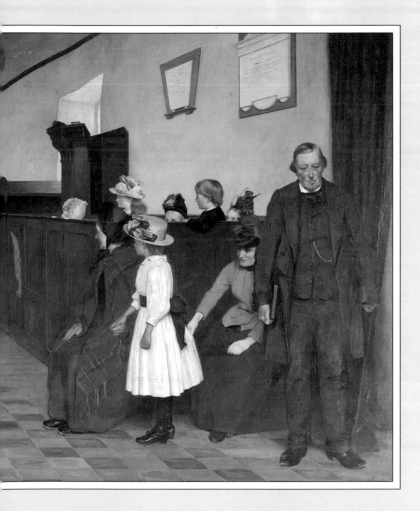

see them made man and wife. But as they drove away later through the lanes, where primroses were peeping and the bleating of lambs came from behind the budding hedges, what groups and groups of smiling faces by cottage-doors gave them respectful good-wishes, and how many bunches of sweet violets were flung into the carriage by the children's hands.

FROM *VIOLET VYVIAN BROWN* BY MAY CROMMELIN AND J. MORAY BROWN

STAR-CROSSED LOVERS

    Friar Laurence So smile the heavens upon this holy act,
That after-hours with sorrow chide us not!
    Romeo Amen, amen! but come what sorrow can,
It cannot countervail the exchange of joy
That one short minute gives me in her sight:

Do thou but close our hands with holy words,
Then love-devouring death do what he dare,
It is enough I may but call her mine.

Friar These violent delights have violent ends,
And in their triumph die! like fire and powder,
Which, as they kiss, consume: The sweetest honey
Is loathsome in his own deliciousness,
And in the taste confounds the appetite:
Therefore, love moderately: long love doth so;
Too swift arrives as tardy as too slow.

ENTER JULIET
Here comes the lady: – O, so light a foot
Will ne'er wear out the everlasting flint:
A lover may bestride the gossamers
That idle in the wanton summer air,
And yet not fall; so light is vanity.

Juliet Good even to my ghostly confessor.

Friar Romeo shall thank thee, daughter, for
us both.

Juliet As much to him, else are his thanks too much.

Romeo Ah, Juliet, if the measure of thy joy
Be heap'd like mine, and that thy skill be more
To blazon it, then sweeten with thy breath
This neighbour air, and let rich musick's tongue
Unfold the imagin'd happiness that both
Receive in either by this dear encounter.

Juliet Conceit, more rich in matter than in words,
Brags of his substance, not of ornament:
They are but beggars that can count their worth;
But my true love is grown to such excess,
I cannot sum up half my sum of wealth.

Friar Come, come with me, and we will make short work;
For, by your leaves, you shall not stay alone,
Till holy church incorporate two in one.

FROM *ROMEO AND JULIET* BY WILLIAM SHAKESPEARE, 1564-1616

THE NEW YEAR WEDDING

A LOVELIER morning never shone upon this world than Karen Wood's wedding morning. There was not a cloud in the sky and the sun shone gloriously through the south windows of the Church upon the brilliant green moss and the Christmas roses and the snowdrops and the laurustinus, the ivy and the fern, and lighted up the old Church into beauty, and touched the brilliant scarlet berries of the holly and its glossy dark, green leaves. Dear Karen. I'm so glad it was so fine, for her sake. The red altar cloth was edged with a double border of ivy leaves, which partly concealed its scanty dimensions and its sad moth-eaten state. Mary Knight was shocked, and said she would prepare her brother Jacob, the parish Churchwarden, for a demand for a new altar cloth.

My Mother was the first of the invited guests to arrive and at the report of a carriage and a pair of greys at the gate the decorations were finished in a hurry, the last touch given, the last leaf picked up or swept away under the great Church chest and all was order and expectation. Fannie and Bessie Little appeared next, having adventurously walked over from Lanhill 4½ miles round by the turnpike road. They did not go to the breakfast, but walked back again directly the wedding was over, as they were invited to spend the *evening* at Langley Green.

Next came the tall bridegroom attended by his two brothers and Arthur Wood. Then Mrs. Wood and little Edward who had tried his best to put off the wedding. He cannot bear the thought of parting with Karen and I don't wonder for she had been a good and loving sister to him, and more than a sister, mother and sister too.

A few minutes after the bride came up the aisle leaning on her father's arm and looking under her veil delicate but lovelier than ever after her illness. The three bridesmaids, the bride's sisters, Ellen, Margaret and Catherine were prettily dressed in pink. Margaret is magnificently lovely.

FROM *THE DIARY OF REVEREND FRANCIS KILVERT*, 1840-1879

BRIDAL BALLAD

*T*HE ring is on my hand,
 And the wreath is on my brow ;
Satins and jewels grand
Are all at my command,
 And I am happy now.

EDGAR ALLAN POE, 1809-1849

AN EPITHALAMION ON THE LADY
ELIZABETH

WHY virgin's girdle now untie,
    And in thy nuptial bed (love's altar) lie
    A pleasing sacrifice ; now dispossess
Thee of these chains and robes which were put on
T'adorn the day, not thee ; for thou, alone,
    Like virtue and truth, art best in nakedness ;
    This bed is only to virginity
A grave, but, to a better state, a cradle ;
Till now thou wast but able
    To be what now thou art ; then that by thee
No more be said, *I may be*, but, *I am*,
Tonight put on perfection, and a woman's name.

JOHN DONNE, 1572-1631

SECOND THOUGHTS

ANCY Coulcher was married the next day. It was not a
gay wedding, though the preparations were perfect,
and no expense had been spared.

The bride in her white looked whiter than any one
remembered to have ever seen her, with red rims round her
eyes, and that pretty pathetic droop about the corners of her
mouth that had touched Douglas Craik, that had touched all
her lovers.

Nobody knew, at least none of the wedding guests knew,
that there had been a little scene before she went to church,

which explained her unusual paleness, and those red rims round her eyes.

Just before she went to church, when she was fully dressed, and the carriages were waiting at the door, and the men were putting the wedding favours in their button-holes, Nancy had broken down in a sudden wild passion of weeping, and had torn off her wreath and veil, and vowed she would not marry Mr. Asquith after all.

Augusta came in in her bridesmaid's gown and found her on her knees beside Lucy's bed.

Lucy had been too ill to get up that morning; she awoke with a splitting headache, and was shut up in a darkened room with wet bandages round her head, and Nancy had come in in all her bridal finery, and had broken down.

She had seized Lucy's hot hands in hers and was imploring her to tell her what to do when Augusta came in.

"Oh, what shall I do, Lucy? what shall I do?" she moaned. "I can't marry Mr. Asquith, indeed I can't marry him!"

Lucy did not know how to answer her. "It is too late to draw back now," she said softly, "you – you should have thought of that before."

FROM *A TRAGIC HONEYMOON* BY ALAN ST AUBYN

SEVEN STEPS

*W*E have taken the seven steps. You have become mine forever. Yes, we have become partners. I have become yours. Hereafter, I cannot live without you. Do not live without me. Let us share the joys. We are word and meaning, united. You are thought and I am sound.

May the nights be honey-sweet for us; may the mornings be honey-sweet for us; may the the earth be honey-sweet for us; may the heavens be honey-sweet for us.

May the plants be honey-sweet for us; may the sun be all honey for us; may the cows yield us honey-sweet milk!

As the heavens are stable, as the earth is stable, as the mountains are stable, as the whole universe is stable, so may our union be permanently settled.

FROM *THE HINDU MARRIAGE RITUAL*

On The Marriage of T.K. and C.C.
The Morning Stormy

*S*UCH should this day be, so the sun should hide
His bashful face, and let the conquering Bride
Without a rival shine, whilst he forbears
To mingle his unequal beams with hers;
Or if sometimes he glance his squinting eye
Between the parting clouds, 'tis but to spy,
Not emulate her glories, so comes dressed
In veils, but as a masquer to the feast.
Thus heaven should lower, such stormy gusts should blow
Not to denounce ungentle Fates, but show
The cheerful Bridegroom to the clouds and wind
Hath all his tears, and all his sighs assigned.
Let tempests struggle in the air, but rest
Eternal calms within thy peaceful breast,
Thrice happy Youth; but ever sacrifice
To that fair hand that dried thy blubbered eyes,
That crowned thy head with roses, and turned all
The plagues of love into a cordial,
When first it joined her virgin snow to thine,
Which when today the Priest shall recombine,
From the mysterious holy touch such charms
Will flow, as shall unlock her wreathèd arms,
And open a free passage to that fruit
Which thou hast toiled for with a long pursuit.
But ere thou feed, that thou may'st better taste
Thy present joys, think on thy torments past.
Think on the mercy freed thee, think upon
Her virtues, graces, beauties, one by one,
So shalt thou relish all, enjoy the whole
Delights of her fair body, and pure soul.
Then boldly to the night of love proceed,
'Tis mercy not to pity though she bleed,
We'll strew no nuts, but change that ancient form,
For till tomorrow we'll prorogue this storm,
Which shall confound with its loud whistling noise
Her pleasing shrieks, and fan thy panting joys.

THOMAS CAREW, 1598-1639

— 72 —

MRS. BEETON'S WEDDING CAKE

*I*NGREDIENTS. – 3½ lb of the finest flour, 3 lb of fresh
butter, 7½ lb of currants, 3 lb of castor sugar, 2 grated
nutmegs, ¼ oz of mace, ¾ of an oz. of cloves, 24 eggs, 1 lb
of sweet whole blanched almonds, ½ a lb of candied citron,
¾ of a lb. each of candied orange- and lemon-peel, 1 gill of
brandy.

METHOD. – Take some good strong household flour and rub
it through a fine sieve on to a sheet of paper. Well wash, dry
and pick the currants, and lay them on the table ready for
use. Blanch the almonds, shred the peel very fine, and mix it
with the currants. Break the eggs, taking especial care to
eliminate any that are bad or musty, and put them into a
clean basin. Weigh the sugar and roll it on the table with a
rolling-pin to break up all lumps; put it in a large pan, add
the butter and all the spices in fine powder, and proceed to
beat the mixture up to a light cream with the hand; add the
eggs 2 at a time, allowing an interval of at least 5 minutes
between each addition of eggs, beating as hard as possible all
the time. When all the eggs have been put in, mix in the fruit
and peel, and last of all add the flour, with the brandy. When
thoroughly well mixed, put it out into well-papered hoops
and press it down in the centre with the back of the hand,
set it into a cool oven and bake for about 6 hours. This
recipe will make about 24 lb of cake, but if a fairly large
oven is not available, it would be better not to bake the
whole of this quantity in 1 hoop, or it will not make
a very satisfactory cake, as the top and sides will
be burnt and dried before the cake can be properly
cooked. It would therefore be preferable to divide
into 2 or more smaller cakes. To ascertain if the cake is
properly cooked, test it with a clean skewer or larding
needle, taking care that the skewer is perfectly clean
and dry; plunge it lightly into the centre of the cake,
and if done the skewer will come out perfectly clean.
On the other hand, according to the quantity and
condition of the paste which adheres to the skewer

the identical state of its rawness can be estimated, and individual judgment must determine how much longer it will require in the oven. As these cakes are better for keeping, it is advisable to make and bake them at least 3 months before they are required. If this is done, the best way to keep them is to strip off all the paper they were baked in, and then to wrap up each cake in a large sheet of rice parchment or wax paper, then wrap it up in several thicknesses of clean newspaper, pack away in a tin or airtight box, and stow away in a dry cool place.

Wedding or Bride's Cakes are thickly encrusted with Almond icing and then iced over with Icing, and when dry are decorated with piping, silver leaves, artificial flowers and gum-paste ornaments. Where something special is desired, natural flowers are used for decoration.

TIME. – To bake, 5 to 6 hours. Sufficient for a 24 lb cake.

FROM *HOUSEHOLD MANAGEMENT* BY *MRS. BEETON*, 1836-1865

ON MY WEDDING-DAY

*H*ERE's a happy new year! but with reason
    I beg you'll permit me to say –
Wish me *many* returns of the *season*.
But as *few* as you please of the day.

January 2, 1820

LORD BYRON, 1788-1824

HONEYMOON

GOING AWAY

*S*OAMES, moving to the well of the staircase, saw
June go, and drew a breath of satisfaction. Why
didn't Fleur come? They would miss their train.
That train would bear her away from him, yet he could
not help fidgeting at the thought that they would lose
it. And then she did come, running down in her
tan-coloured frock and black velvet cap, and passed
him into the drawing-room. He saw her kiss her
mother, her aunt, Val's wife, Imogen, and then come
forth, quick and pretty as ever. How would she treat
him at this last moment of her girlhood? He couldn't
hope for much!

Her lips pressed the middle of his cheek.

"Daddy!" she said, and was past and gone. Daddy!
She hadn't called him that for years. He drew a long
breath and followed slowly down. There was all the
folly with that confetti stuff and the rest of it to go
through with, yet. But he would like just to catch her
smile, if she leaned out, though they would hit her in
the eye with the shoe, if they didn't take care. Young
Mont's voice said fervently in his ear:

"Good-bye, sir; and thank you! I'm so fearfully
bucked."

"Good-bye," he said; "don't miss your train."

He stood on the bottom step but three, whence he
could see above the heads – the silly hats and heads.
They were in the car now; and there was that stuff,
showering, and there went the shoe. A flood of
something welled up in Soames, and – he didn't know –
he couldn't see!

FROM *THE FORSYTE SAGA* BY JOHN GALSWORTHY. 1867-1933

SONG

*T*wo wedded lovers watched the rising moon,
   That with her strange mysterious beauty glowing,
   Over misty hills and waters flowing,
Crowned the long twilight loveliness of June:
   And thus in me, and thus in me, they spake,
   The solemn secret of first love did wake.

Above the hills the blushing orb arose;
   Her shape encircled by a radiant bower,
   In which the nightingale with charmèd power
Poured forth enchantment o'er the dark repose:
   And thus in me, and thus in me, they said,
   Earth's mists did with the sweet new spirit wed.

Far up the sky with ever purer beam,
   Upon the throne of night the moon was seated,
   And down the valley glens the shades retreated,
And silver light was on the open stream.
   And thus in me, and thus in me, they sighed,
   Aspiring Love has hallowed Passion's tide.

GEORGE MEREDITH, 1828-1909

CHARITY ROYALL

AN HOUR later, coming out of the glare of the dining-room, she waited in the marble-panelled hall while Mr. Royall, before the brass lattice of one of the corner counters, selected a cigar and bought an evening paper. Men were lounging in rocking chairs under the blazing chandeliers, travellers coming and going, bells ringing, porters shuffling by with luggage. . . .

Charity stood among these cross-currents of life as motionless and inert as if she had been one of the tables screwed to the marble floor. All her soul was gathered up into one sick sense of coming doom, and she watched Mr. Royall in fascinated terror while he pinched the cigars in successive boxes and unfolded his evening paper with a steady hand.

Presently he turned and joined her. "You go right along up to bed – I'm going to sit down here and have my smoke," he said. He spoke as easily and naturally as if they had been an old couple, long used to each other's ways, and her contracted heart gave a flutter of relief.

FROM *SUMMER* BY EDITH WHARTON, 1862-1937

HONEYMOON

*A*ND when they came out of the lace shop there was
their own driver and the cab they called their own cab
waiting for them under a plane tree. What luck!
Wasn't it luck? Fanny pressed her husband's arm. These
things seemed always to be happening to them ever since they
– came abroad. Didn't he think so too? But George stood on
the pavement edge, lifted his stick, and gave a loud "Hi!"
Fanny sometimes felt a little uncomfortable about the way
George summoned cabs, but the drivers didn't seem to mind,
so it must have been all right. Fat, good-natured, and smiling,
they stuffed away the little newspaper they were reading,
whipped the cotton cover off the horse, and were ready to
obey.

"I say," George said as he helped Fanny in, "suppose we
go and have tea at the place where the lobsters grow. Would
you like to?"

"Most awfully," said Fanny fervently, as she leaned back
wondering why the way George put things made them sound
so very nice.

"R-right, *bien.*" He was beside her. "*Allay,*" he cried gaily,
and off they went.

Off they went, spanking along lightly, under the green and
gold shade of the plane trees, through the small streets that
smelled of lemons and fresh coffee, past the fountain square
where women, with water-pots lifted, stopped talking to gaze
after them, round the corner past the café, with its pink and
white umbrellas, green tables, and blue siphons, and so to the
sea front. There a wind, light, warm, came flowing over the
boundless sea. It touched George, and Fanny it seemed to
linger over while they gazed at the dazzling water. And
George said, "Jolly, isn't it?" And Fanny, looking dreamy,
said, as she said at least twenty times a day since they – came
abroad: "Isn't is extraordinary to think that here we are
quite alone, away from everybody, with nobody to tell us to
go home, or to – to order us about except ourselves?"

FROM *THE DOLL'S HOUSE* BY KATHERINE MANSFIELD, 1888-1923

BRIDAL SONG

O COME, soft rest of cares! come, Night!
  Come, naked Virtue's only tire,
The reapèd harvest of the light
Bound up in sheaves of sacred fire.
    Love calls to war :
      Sighs his alarms,
    Lips his swords are,
      The field his arms.

Come, Night, and lay thy velvet hand
  On glorious Day's outfacing face ;
And all thy crownèd flames command
  For torches to our nuptial grace.
    Love calls to war :
      Sighs his alarms,
    Lips his swords are,
      The field his arms.

GEORGE CHAPMAN, 1559-1634

CLAUDINE'S WEDDING NIGHT

*I*N THE Rue de Bassano, I hardly caught more than a glimpse of that flat "too like an eighteenth-century engraving" that he had hitherto refused to let me enter. The only light came from shaded writing-lamps placed on the tables. To intoxicate myself still more, I breathed in that smell of light tobacco and Russian leather that permeates Renaud's clothes and his long moustache.

I seem to be still there, I can see myself, I *am* there.

So, the moment had come? What should I do? For a split second, I thought of Luce. Without realising it, I removed my hat. I took my loved one's hand to reassure myself and I gazed at him. Carelessly, he threw off his hat and gloves and drew back a little, with a trembling sigh. I looked lovingly at his beautiful dark eyes and his arched nose and his faded gold hair that the wind had artfully ruffled. I went up close to him, but he retreated mischievously and contemplated me from a little distance, while all my splendid courage drained away. I clasped my hands.

"Oh! Please do be quick!"

Alas, I did not realise how funny that remark was.

He sat down.

"Come here, Claudine."

Sitting on his knees, he could hear that I was breathing too fast; his voice became tender.

"Are you my very own?"

"You know I am. I've been yours for so long."

"You're not frightened?"

"No; I'm not frightened. To begin with, I know everything!"

"What, everything?"

He slid me down, so that I lay on his knees, and bent over my mouth. I put up no defence and let his lips drink deep.

FROM *CLAUDINE MARRIED* BY COLETTE, 1873-1954

— 88 —

FRIENDSHIP IN MARRIAGE

ONCE or twice, in the first days of his marriage, he had asked himself with a slight shiver what would happen if Susy should begin to bore him. The thing had happened to him with other women as to whom his first emotions had not differed in intensity from those she inspired. The part he had played in his previous love-affairs might indeed have been summed up in the memorable line: "I am the hunter and the prey," for he had invariably ceased to be the first only to regard himself as the second. This experience had never ceased to cause him the liveliest pain, since his sympathy for his pursuer was only less keen than his commiseration for himself; but as he was always a little sorrier for himself, he had always ended by distancing the pursuer.

All these pre-natal experiences now seemed utterly inapplicable to the new man he had become. He could not imagine being bored by Susy – or trying to escape from her if he were. He could not think of her as an enemy, or even as an accomplice, since accomplices are potential enemies: she was some one with whom, by some unheard-of miracle, joys above the joys of friendship were to be tasted, but who, even through these fleeting ecstasies, remained simply and securely his friend.

FROM *THE GLIMPSES OF THE MOON* BY EDITH WHARTON, 1862-1937

A Glow of Happiness

*B*UT, in spite of these depressing possibilities, she particularly wanted to have a few, a very few, people down for that Sunday. They had all a special connection with Bray. Things had happened there before, and it was a party of healed memories that was to gather there. If, after all, the weather turned out to be hopelessly unpropitious, they could all sit in a ring round the fire, holding each other's hands. She felt sure they would like to do that. Probably there would be a great many *tête-à-têtes* in various corners, or, if it were warm, in various punts. But she felt sure that they would all hold hands in the intervals of these.

Jeannie and Victor had been married in the autumn, and since then they had practically disappeared, surrounded by a glow of their own happiness. They had sunk below the horizon, but from the horizon there had, so to speak, come up a brilliant illumination like an aurora borealis.

But Lady Nottingham considered that they had aurora-ed quite long enough. They had no right to keep all their happiness to themselves; it was their duty to diffuse it, and let other people warm their hands and hearts at it. She had written what is diplomatically known as a "strong note" to say so, and she had mentioned that she was not alone in considering that they were being rather selfish.

FROM *DAISY'S AUNT* BY E.F. BENSON, 1867-1940

A Sense of Belonging

ONSONBY had been a rather pretty, but pale and somewhat peevish-looking girl; but Mrs. Crosbie was round and rosy and smiling, as if she had never known a care in the wide world.

"How well you are looking!" exclaimed Joan, as they met. "Why, I should hardly have known you again. Italy has worked miracles for you, Cecily. I have never seen you look so rosy before!"

"Oh, it isn't Italy," replied the bride, as she kissed unwilling Joan over and over again; "it's my Charlie, Miss Trevor. He's been so good to me, that my honeymoon has been a species of Paradise. I've been telling all the girls this afternoon to get married as soon as ever they can. They won't know what life is until they do!"

"But they might not get another Captain Crosbie," said Joan, laughing.

"No," replied Cecily, pursing her lips; "I suppose not; for I don't believe there can be two men like him in the world. But still they can get good men to love them; and what I mean is that they must not let a chance go by."

"I dare say you are right," said Joan, musingly, "and that mutual love is the best thing we can attain."

"Oh, it isn't only the love, dear!" replied Mrs. Crosbie, who seemed to have grown marvellously wise since they had parted. "Many people love, you know, and are very miserable in consequence; it's the beautiful security and freedom in marriage that makes it so happy. To feel that you actually *belong* to your husband – that you have a right to appeal to him for advice or assistance or protection whenever you require it; that all the world may know you love each other and you may glory in the fact – I think that is the grand thing that brings so much peace and pleasure with it!"

"But cannot one love in secret and feel just as happy?" questioned Joan. "Isn't there something more sacred in a private love that is not shared by the world?"

Mrs. Crosbie thought a moment and then shook her head.

FROM *A RATIONAL MARRIAGE* BY FLORENCE MARRYAT, 1838-1899

A May Morning

UT though night is good, and stars are good, and sweet communion is very good, with one's beloved lying soft and warm in one's arms, day also is good, and the stir and zest of it, and men's voices, and the wind along the heath.

Such were Christopher's conclusions when he had been married a week. He leant on the gate after breakfast on the first weekly anniversary of his wedding day, smoking and gazing at the field of buttercups that so gorgeously embroidered the edges of the sea, and reflected that you have to have both – the blissful night, the active day, so as completely to appreciate either. That is, if your life is to be as near perfect as possible. And why shouldn't his life be as near perfect as possible? It had all the necessary ingredients – youth, health, and Catherine. Only, for a day to be happy it must not be too much like the night; there must be a contrast, and there must be a complete contrast. In the days and nights of the last week there had been hardly any contrast, and wasn't contrast in life as indispensable as salt in cooking? Bliss there had been, bliss in quantities, wonderful quantities; wild bliss, then quiet bliss, then wild bliss again, then quiet bliss, but always bliss. He adored Catherine. Life was marvellous. On that fine May morning he was certain he was the happiest human being in the island, for nobody could possibly be happier, nor could anybody be as happy, for nobody else had Catherine; but he wished that that day –

Well, what did he wish that day? It wasn't possible that he wanted to be away from Catherine, yet he did want to, – for a

few hours, for a little while; why if only to have the joy of coming back to her. He was conscious, and the consciousness surprised him, that he didn't want to kiss her for a bit. No, he didn't. And fancy not wanting to, when a month ago he would have sold everything he had, including his soul, to be allowed to! That came, thought Christopher, narrowing his eyes to watch a white sail out at sea bending in the wind – Jove, how jolly it looked, scudding along like that – of not having contrast. There had to be interruption, pause, the mind switched off on to something else. How could one ever know the joy of coming back if one didn't first go?

FROM *LOVE* BY ELIZABETH VON ARNIM. 1866-1941

REFLECTIONS

THE HAPPY HUSBAND

OFT, oft methinks, the while with Thee
    I breathe, as from the heart, thy dear
    And dedicated name, I hear
A promise and a mystery,
    A pledge of more than passing life,
    Yea, in that very name of Wife!

S.T. COLERIDGE, 1772-1834

MY WIFE

*T*RUSTY, dusky, vivid, true,
　　With eyes of gold and bramble-dew,
　Steel-true and blade-straight,
The great artificer
Made my mate.

Honour, anger, valour, fire;
A love that life could never tire,
Death quench or evil stir,
The mighty master
Gave to her.

Teacher, tender, comrade, wife,
A fellow-farer true through life,
Heart-whole and soul-free
The august father
Gave to me.

ROBERT LOUIS STEVENSON, 1850-1894

A MATCH

*I*F LOVE were what the rose is,
　　And I were like the leaf,
Our lives would grow together
In sad or singing weather,
Blown fields or flowerful closes,
　　Green pleasure or grey grief ;
If love were what the rose is,
　　And I were like the leaf.

If I were what the words are,
　　And love were like the tune,
With double sound and single
Delight our lips would mingle,
With kisses glad as birds are
　　That get sweet rain at noon ;
If I were what the words are,
　　And love were like the tune.

If you were life, my darling,
　　And I your love were death,
We 'd shine and snow together
Ere March made sweet the weather
With daffodil and starling
　　And hours of fruitful breath ;
If you were life, my darling,
　　And I your love were death.

ALGERNON CHARLES SWINBURNE, 1837-1909

LONGING FOR THE EMPEROR

MY LORD has departed
And the time has grown long.
Shall I search the mountains,
Going forth to meet you,
Or wait for you here?

No! I would not live,
Longing for you,
On the mountain crag, rather,
Rock-root as my pillow,
Dead would I lie.

Yet even if it be so
I shall wait for my Lord,
Till on my black hair –
Trailing fine in the breeze –
The dawn's frost shall fall.

In the autumn field,
Over the rice ears,
The morning mist trails,
Vanishing somewhere . . .
Can my love fade too?

EMPRESS IWA NO HIME, c.300 A.D.

THE GOOD MORROW

I WONDER BY my troth, what thou and I
    Did, till we loved? were we not weaned till then?
But sucked on country pleasures, childishly?
    Or snorted we i'the seven sleepers' den?
'Twas so; But this, all pleasures fancies be.
If ever any beauty I did see,
Which I desired, and got, 'twas but a dream of thee.

And now good morrow to our waking souls,
    Which watch not one another out of fear;
For love, all love of other sights controls,
    And makes one little room, an everywhere.
Let sea-discoverers to new worlds have gone,
Let maps to others, worlds on worlds have shown,
Let us possess our world, each hath one, and is one.

My face in thine eye, thine in mine appears,
    And true plain hearts do in the faces rest,
Where can we find two better hemispheres
    Without sharp North, without declining West?
Whatever dies, was not mixed equally;
If our two loves be one, or, thou and I
Love so alike, that none do slacken, none can die.

JOHN DONNE, 1572-1631

A MARRIAGE RING

*T*HE ring so worn as you behold,
So thin, so pale, is yet of gold :
The passion such it was to prove ;
Worn with life's cares, love yet was love.

GEORGE CRABBE. 1754-1832

PENHALIGON'S ORANGE BLOSSOM

*O*RANGE BLOSSOM, a flower of the gods, was offered by
Jupiter to his beloved Juno on their nuptial day. The
pure white flowers, with their delicate waxy petals, were
traditionally carried by brides in their bouquets or woven
into a crown to adorn their veil. The rich and honied
fragrance of *Orange Blossom*, reminiscent of love and
romance, was created by Penhaligon's for the bride to
celebrate the most special of events, the wedding.

ACKNOWLEDGEMENTS

PICTURE CREDITS:

Art Resource, New York:
p7 *Signing the Register*: Edmund Blair Leighton; p78-79 *Leaving Home*: Edward Henry Lamson.

Birmingham Museum and Art Gallery:
p82 *An English Autumn Afternoon*: Ford Madox Brown.

Bridgeman Art Library, London:
p5 *Her Wedding Day*: Anton Weiss/Christie's, London; p8-9 *Gather Ye Rosebuds While Ye May*: Theodore Blake Wirgman/Bradford Art Galleries and Museums; p10-11 *The Wedding*: V Marais Milton/Eaton Gallery, London; p15 *Trust Me*: John Everett Millais/Forbes Magazine Collection, NY; p18-19 *Ask Me No More*: Sir Lawrence Alma-Tadema/Private Collection; p20 *A Moment's Reflection*: William Henry Margetson/Bonhams, London; p21 *My Next Door Neighbour*: Edmund Blair Leighton/Private Collection; p22 *Jealousy and Flirtation*: Haynes King/V&A; p25 *The Wedding Gown*: John Faed/Christopher Wood Gallery, London; p29 *Lady in Evening Dress*: Henri Thomas/Gavin Graham Gallery, London; p32-33 *The Betrothed*: John William Godward/Guildhall Art Gallery; p34 *At the Window*: Anna Alma-Tadema/Christopher Wood Gallery, London; p37 *A Summer Shower*: Edith Hayllar/Forbes Magazine Collection, NY; p38 *Louis Signorino Seated in his Study*: Gustave Bourgain/Galerie George, London; p39 *Portrait of a Young Woman*: Edmond François Aman-Jean/Musée du Petit Palais, Paris; p40 *The Seamstress*: Charles Baugniet/V&A; p42 *Miss Sybil Walker*: Maurice Greiffenhagen/Whitford and Hughes, London; p43 *The Wedding Dress*: George Goodwin Kilburne/Phillips, Fine Art Auctioneers; p44-45 *The Wedding Meal*: Albert-Auguste Fourie/Musée des Beaux-Arts, Rouen; p50 *A Village Wedding*: John White/Royal Albert Memorial Museum, Exeter; p52-53 *The Village Wedding*: Sir Luke Fildes/Christie's, London; p57 *Till Death Us Do Part*: Edmund Blair Leighton/Forbes Magazine Collection, NY; p58 *James Silk Buckingham and his Wife* (detail): H W Pickersgill/Royal Geographical Society; p60-61 *Happy is the Bride the Sun Shines On*: James Hayllar/Atkinson Art Gallery, Southport, Lancs; p65 *Signing the Marriage Register*: James Charles/Bradford Art Galleries and Museums; p66 *Fresh from the Altar*: Jessica Hayllar/Christie's, London; p68 *Woman in an Interior*: Albert Breaute/Gavin Graham Gallery, London; p70 *Radha and Krishna on a Bed*: Punjab Hills/V&A; p71 *A Rajput Prince and his Mistress Painted at Burdi*: Private Collection; p75 *The Wedding Breakfast*: F D Hardy/Atkinson Art Gallery, Southport, Lancs; p80-81 *The Only Daughter*: Jessica Hayllar/Forbes Magazine Collection, NY; p83 *La Mondaine*: James Jacques Tissot/Joey & Toby Tanenbaum Collection, Toronto; p84-85 *The Restaurant*: Russian School/Tretjakoff Galerie, Moscow; p86-87 *Signor Marsilio and his Wife*: Lorenzo Lotto/Prado, Madrid; p91 *The Honeymoon*: Robert Hannah/Rafael Valls Gallery, London; p93 *The Garden of Eden*: Hugh Goldwyn Riviere/Guildhall Art Gallery; p95 *Au Café*: Fernand Toussaint/Whitford and Hughes, London; p96 *Cornfield in the Isle of Wight* (detail): Richard Burchett/V&A; p97 *Nordic Summer Evening*: Sven Richard Bergh/Goteborgs Konstmuseum, Sweden; p101 *Lady with a Cat*: Charles Massard/Waterhouse and Dodd, London; p105 *A Chinese Girl Seated Looking Out of a Window*: Attributed to Lam Qua/Christie's London; p108 *Mrs Wilton Phipps* (detail): John Singer Sargent/Private Collection.

Cleveland Museum of Art, Ohio:
p73 *A Bridal Pair*: Anon. Delia E Holden and L E Holden Funds.

Fine Art Photographic Archive, London:
p13 *By Unfrequented Ways*: William Henry Gore; p27 *An Arabian Fantasy*:
Abbey Alston; p69 *The Wedding Toast*: Erik Henningsen.

Manchester City Art Galleries: p109 *Girl Reading*: Charles Edward Perugini.

Museo De Arte De Ponce, Luis Ferré Foundation, Puerto Rico:
p48-49 *Flaming June*: Frederick, Lord Leighton.

Museum of Fine Arts, Boston:
p98-99 *The Painter's Honeymoon*: Frederick, Lord Leighton.

National Galleries of Scotland: p16 *The Letter of Introduction*: David Wilkie.

National Museums and Galleries on Merseyside. Lady Lever Art Gallery:
p3 *The Wedding Morning*: J H F Bacon.

Photographie Giraudon, Paris:
p42 *Spring*: Sir John Lavery/Musée D'Orsay, Paris; p107 *Francesca da Rimini
and Paulo Malaterta*: Jean Auguste Dominique Ingres/Musée des Beaux Arts,
Angers.

Private Collection: p100 *The Proposal*: William Powell Frith.

Reproduced by Gracious Permission of Her Majesty The Queen:
p47 *Bianca*: Frederick, Lord Leighton.

Reproduced by Gracious Permission of Her Majesty Queen Elizabeth, The Queen
Mother: p30-31 *The Eve of Saint Agnes*: Sir John Everett Millais.

Reproduced by Kind Permission of the Principal, Fellows and Scholars of Jesus
College, Oxford: p59 *New College Cloisters*: William Holman Hunt.

Royal Academy of Arts, London: p67 *Vanity*: Frank Cadogan Cowper.

Sotheby's, London: p23 *Sylvia*: Sir Frank Dicksee.

Southampton City Art Gallery: p62 *Romeo and Juliet*: Sir Frank Dicksee.

Tate Gallery, London:
p55 *Pamela is Married*: Joseph Highmore; p76-77 *The Health of the Bride*:
Stanhope Forbes; p89 *Portrait*: James Jacques Tissot; p103 *Harmony*: Sir Frank
Dicksee.

Cover: *Spring*: Sir John Lavery: Musée D'Orsay/Photographie Giraudon, Paris.

TEXT CREDITS:

p37 *A Room with a View* by E M Forster. UK © Edward Arnold Publishers;
USA © Alfred A Knopf Inc.
p88 *Claudine Married* by Colette. Translation © 1960, 1988 by Martin, Secker and
Warburg, Ltd. Reprinted by permission of Farrar, Straus and Giroux, Inc.;
UK © Secker and Warburg, Ltd.
p104 *Longing for the Emperor* by Empress Iwa no Hime, from *The Penguin Book
of Japanese Verse* translated by Geoffrey Bownas and Anthony Thwaite
(Penguin Books, 1964), © Geoffrey Bownas and Anthony Thwaite, 1964.

Designed by Bernard Higton
Picture research by Lynda Marshall

Published in the United States by Harmony Books,
a division of Crown Publishers, Inc.,
201 East 50th Street, New York, New York 10022

Published in Great Britain by Pavilion Books Limited

HARMONY and colophon are trademarks of
Crown Publishers, Inc.

Manufactured in Hong Kong by Imago

ISBN 0-517-58507-3

Library of Congress Cataloging-in-Publication Data
A Bridal Bouquet/[edited by] Sheila Pickles
       p. cm.
    1. Marriage customs and rites. 2. Wedding etiquette.
I. Pickles, Sheila.
GT2690.875   1991   91-10742
392'.5--dc20   CIP

10 9 8 7 6 5 4 3 2 1

First American Edition